BREAST

BREAST

CLAIRR O'CONNOR

ASTROLABE
2004

COPYRIGHT 2004
BY CLAIRR O'CONNOR

ISBN 0-9548580-0-X

CONDITIONS OF SALE
This book is sold subject to the condition
that it shall not, by way of trade or other-
wise, be lent, re-sold, hired out or otherwise
circulated without the publisher's prior
consent in any form of binding or cover
other than that in which it is published and
without a similar condition including this
condition being imposed on the subsequent
purchaser.

Astrolabe Press
PO Box No. 9837,
Dublin 8

This book
is for every woman
who battles breast cancer

ACKNOWLEDGEMENTS

Acknowledgements are due to the editors of the following publications where some of these poems, or earlier versions of them, have appeared:
Poetry Ireland Review; *The White Page/An Bhilleog Bhan*: Twentieth Century Irish Women Poets (Ed. Joan McBreen);
On The Counterscarp, Limerick Writing, 1961 - 1991, (Eds. Anthony O'Brien, Ciaran O'Driscoll, Jo Slade, Mark Whelan), Fourfront Poets and Salmon Publishing;
Under Brigid's Cloak, (Ed. Sheila O'Hagan) *Home*, an Anthology of Modern Irish Writing, (Ed. Siobhan Parkinson), A and A Farmar, 1996; *RTE Radio One*; *Writing Women*, Vol. 11, No. 3, Vol. 12, No. 1 (Newcastle upon Tyne, England); *Podium*, Samhlaiocht Chiarrai;
Stony Thursday Book; *Women's Studies*, Claremount Graduate University, Calif. Vol. 31, No. 4.

CONTENTS
Section One
Breasts

Agatha	13
This Year	14
Putti Pull Hair	15
Nightmares	
1 Vision	16
2. Heads	16
3. Beadbones	17
Hospital	18
What They Say	20
Vanished Words (After Chemo)	21
Laboratory (MRN 0706592)	2
Radiation	23
Bed	24
Wake Me	25
Palimpsest	26
El Greco	28
Nightmares	
4. Gunfire	29
5. Erased	29
Incipit	31
Nightmare	
6. Hermitage	32
My Good Right Hand	34
Eamon's Dragons	37
Missing	38
The Hammock	40
Mute	42

Section Two
Daughterhood

Confined	47
Blinds	49
Slower	50
White Scars	51
Silent Hands	52
The Piano	53
Runaway Girl	55
Cobwebs	62
Her Hands	63
My Hands	64
Interval Act	65
Lent	66
Home Economics	67
Cookbooks and Soap	68
Mama at Rest	70
Eyrie	71

BREASTS

AGATHA

Her face was ecstatically removed.

The picture showed two Roman soldiers
smiling as they presented her
with a platter holding her breasts.
Their swords dripped blood.

The ecclesiastical calendar hung
in my childhood kitchen,
my birthday shared with St Agatha.

The surgeon's mannered formality distances
the news somehow, as if he's
presenting a telegram on a salver
to someone else.

After his knife has
cut and scraped--
fifty-five staples
shining like some strange xylophone.
Touch.
You can almost beat out breast music
to the heart's allegro.

Now my hospital corner blooms
with lilies, begonias, roses.
Their colours beckon and reassure.
They bloom up my arm,
suddenly black, mauve, blue.

I carried belladonnas
in my twenty year old hand
my new-married mouth a red flower of such happiness;
the lilies, loftily pure.

These roses, so much blood lost.

THIS YEAR

This year started with the wheeze
of last year's end.
Your caged breath punctuated
Christmas while I read you
Middlemarch.
Now, it is Spring.
Your breathing is regular
as I measure night.
Your back's gone though.
You sleep with a pillow
babied between your knees.
My head swims to your breathing.
Morning is a lifetime away.

My mind refuses:
too many facts in small print.
The ghoul watchers
who weigh me with their eyes.
My new identity
MRN 0706592.
People who tell
me I am fine.
Crowded waiting rooms.
Interrogative phonecalls

PUTTI PULL HAIR

Hair and head ache now
day and night.

It comes out
on my brush, pillow, shoulders.
Bald patches grow to meet each other,
an accelerated crazy tonsure.

One night I wake from the terrors
of Titian putti swinging from
my locks, the prize of my red-gold
squeezed in their padded palms.

The pain pulls me to myself.

NIGHTMARES

1. Vision

I was about to ask
a question only to
discover my mouth
was zipped shut.

Opened, a torrent
of pens fell out.

So many?
Who would have thought
that one small mouth could hold etc?

Now, free to scream,
I cling to silence
focus my partial
vision at floor level.
I piece together
one of my walking boots--
relaxed, tongue lolling,
on its side.

2. Heads

I'm in an alabaster house,
cobwebs, creaky floorboards,
dust settling at starlight.

I open a door into a room,
feel movement under my feet.

The floor is made up
of moving bald heads.
Too many eyes look up
at me.
The floor,
multiples of my head.

3. Bead Bones

How could it be!
I was stringing a perfect
bead bone necklace from
my own skeleton.

I had diminutive silver
instruments to form the bead
bones into delicate shapes.

My skeleton disarticulated
as the work progressed.
I was very pleased with myself.

HOSPITAL

I have waited so long I am a mannequin.
Personality and temperament rubbed clean.
My shiny head is wigged—
my eyes, a smudge without eyebrows.

My limbs have stiffened in resistance.
Poke me—my rigid right hand will point
in the direction you desire.
Lift me up.
I won't complain.

Call my name.
I may not answer.

******

You know that you're not
just one breast.
You know you're not
a bald head
though it seems
to take up the sky
when you go outdoors.

You know you're not
just a Picc line
into which the chemo toxins
flow.
But each week
they dance in your veins
sleep overwhelms you.

You know you're not
an object when two nurses
arrange you on the too high
chrome slab for the bright
sun of radium,
your hands bent in a
contortionist's unbearable dance.

WHAT THEY SAY

It won't be half as bad
as you imagine.

You look grand.
Try not to get depressed.

Any one of us could be
killed going under a bus.

The doctors don't know
everything.

You're strong. You'll
get over this.

Old age is overrated
and expensive.

Don't worry about losing your hair,
you've always looked good in hats.

If we all gave in to anxiety,
where would we be?

You're lucky. They can
cure your cancer, but I'm
still suicidal.

VANISHED WORDS
(AFTER CHEMO)

1.

A morning came when I was
looking for simple words
I couldn't find.

I moved from room to room
as if I might find a clue
in the curve of a chair
or a vase of blown tulips.

Body in agitato.
Head not in charge.
You, not there.

2.

It's lunchtime.
We talk and talk now.
Your words, a waterfall of love,
mine, a staccato stuttering
in response.

Last night, I cast
the bedclothes aside
and walked the navy night
still looking.

But it takes another day
before the right words land
lightly as a feather.
Then I realize, silence
is a language too.

LABORATORY
(MRN *0706592*)

Fill this, answer that,
tell us what you feel.

Tell us but not too much
just what we need for this
Quality of Life questionnaire.

There are bloods.
Always bloods—coming out
or going in.

Extend your hand
in the preferred manner.

What's happened to your veins?
Are you disappointed in your body?
To what extent were you interested in sex?
Did you ever work in the Social Services?

Not at all. A little. Quite a bit. Very Much.

RADIATION

Laid out, ready for gutting,
one hand stirruped backwards
above my head, the other
painfully laid to specific
measurements by my side
but at an awkward curve.

I'm told to lie still
by the team of radiotherapy nurses
as they leave the room
to zap me in the right places
with their technology.

They return, adjust me
according to numbers they cite
at each other.
Leave again and zap.

And so it goes on
the radiation waltz.
In, out and in again.

When it's done
the nurse does a tap
dance with the release button
on the slab.
I'm lowered to a normal level
and exert myself to my feet.

It's goodbye until tomorrow
when we waltz again.

BED

I hold the newly bought coverlet
back in invitation.

Its colours and textures
warm this winter night.
Velvets and silks welcome you.
So many colours—
cerise, deep blue, green,
gold, orange, purple.

Each dark velvet panel
boasts intermittent gold orbs.
They shine like some invented
sky now.
Last night, they watched
the black hours with me.

Come my love, let me warm you.
See, you can feel my heat
when I'm turned towards you.

You gently touch the hollowed place
It's decorated with the cerise
markings of the radiotherapy nurse—
crosses and dots, crazily festive.

You kiss their route.

WAKE ME

Wake me with a cooing in the ear,
a rub on the forehead,
a full-mouthed kiss.

Tell me I'm beautiful
though I know I never was.
Sing to me though you've told me
 you never had a voice.

I have no Magdalene hair
to wipe anything away.
Now all is translucent in our glass house.
Tell me I'm the only jewel you want.

Assure me those toxins pouring
through me are a honeyed well.
Feed me fruits at dawn —
melon, grapes, mango, passion.

Dress me in gorgeous fabrics.
Let me play other parts
in wigs and paints.

Be my lover, father, brother, friend.
Be complicit in all I can be.

PALIMPSEST

(for Kev)

Come, my calligrapher,
see what they've done.

I've become their palimpsest.
That's what my body is now.

It used to be ours.
We wrote on it together.

Decades of lovemaking,
an invisible script
that was ours alone.

How we practised our cadel strokes
with cinnabar!

Come closer.
You'll hardly recognise me.
I don't recognise myself.

See, there's a hollow
where my breast
used to be.

Look at the wound
from my mid-chest around
to my back.
What a flat undecorated line!

My heart is too near
the surface.

Look at my markings.
They've tattooed me—
small dark permanent marks
like Candle Black,
descenders below the wound line.
Dots that map me forever.

Oh, to have my eager
careless body back
to weave a rinceau with you!

EL GRECO

(Mater Dolorosa, 1590's)

The gaze of the Virgin
is upon me—
those liquid brown eyes
hold me.

Her son is dead
but there are no tears.
Her intensity binds me.

A white veil
frames the perfect oval
of her face.
Over this—a cloak
of ultramarine.

She looks too young
to have known the death
of a grown child.

Christ was man
when they took him
from the cross
but there is no sign
of age on her face.

No sunken eyes
or cheeks tracked
by wrinkles.

Just that glance.

NIGHTMARES

4. Gunfire.

Bird droppings stain the entrance
of the derelict house.
Pigeons home there.
Seagulls screech the house awake.
Humidity drags my feet
onto the verandah
to the table laid years ago
and abandoned mid meal.
I preside over the cobwebs
and hand filthy cups and photos to guests
above the sound of gunfire.

"They have sucked the land dry,"
the emaciated old gent says
as he clicks his dentures
"but we won't be moved
despite their chorus of gunfire."

He drinks the cobwebs with relish.

5. Erased

I look through the lace
of the lift cage
as we are rising.
They hold me fast,
my white-robed keepers.

We arrive at the glass penthouse.
Wires trail from my body.
I'm plugged into the motherboard.

"Tell all,"
"Tell some," they hiss.
My resistance builds.

How can I know
what I haven't
let myself know?

They are downloading
my pattern onto a floppy disk.

"Who controls what is reality?"
"We do," they chorus.

I feel the last trace of myself leave me.
My energies will be transferred
to someone else.

I have been scrambled and erased.

INCIPIT

(for Terry Hayden)

I don't know when I could
have said, "Here begins"
my story like a medieval monk.

Mine is a muddled beginning.
A moment I can't name
— except to say it must have been
that second when one epithelial cell
mutated in its DNA
and began dividing.

But a year on after surgery
 I'm looking at pictures in Paris.

A red-haired young woman lies abandoned.
A figure fragments to three breasts.
Another, fleshier, with a fullness that arrests the eye,
lays an extra arm by her side.

I move on and am eyeball to an open vagina,
limbs about it like spare parts.

Discreetly I finger the prosthesis
and adjust my red wig.
I wouldn't want to disturb that man
gawping at the purple vulva.

Then I make my way downwards
to the permanent collection.

NIGHTMARES

6. Hermitage.

I choose a room in the Hermitage.
Its walls of red silk,
its red-wood floor scattered
with the richest of rugs.
Red chandeliers.

A room full of Rembrandts,
red on red on red.
I lie on a red chaise longue.
I watch his old man portraits
hypnotise me until I think I see
from behind and through his eyes.
I luxuriate in redness.

Such warmth.
Even my eyes are red.
My eye - or is it Rembrandt's-
caught on the corner of the silk
wall covering.

Bleeding.
So much blood.
Its stickiness
almost fastens
me to the ground.

I hurl myself at walls
no longer able to see clearly.
I swallow some mouthfuls.

Almost resign myself
to drowning when a door
gives way to a room
so completely white,
I'm blinded for some moments.

At first it seems a room
of windows and couches.
A white rug merges into
indistinguishable space.
But as my vision clears

I see a transparent ice-house
and choose to rest in that.
All stickiness is gone.

I'm all white
in a transparent
ice-house
in a
white room.

MY GOOD RIGHT HAND

(for Jo Slade)

Today I face the sea.
I can see it rushing
towards me as I sit
in bed reading
in this holiday cottage.

Too frail to walk too far
today.
I tramped too many miles
yesterday –
my legs creak their legacy.

While I'm looking at a 17th century
self-portrait by Judith Leyster,
a coven of crows
make quick work
of yesterday's leftovers
we put on the altar
of railway sleepers and stone,
the sturdy outdoor table
for summer feasts.
Too early for outdoor idylls yet.

Judith looks directly at me
as if taking a break from
the portrait she's painting.
It's a fiddler dressed
in a blue cap and shirt.

She looks self-assured
as she gazes at me or
anyone else who might look
at her—
her painting hand resting
in this interrupted moment

yet she still holds her paintbrush.
Her cap and collar ruff
a perfect starched white.

I tell her about
my bloated body,
steroid thick,
my lymphoedemic left hand
dragging me earthwards
in perpetual off-balance.

I imagine her painting
the hollowed woundline
where my left breast
used to be
as we chat about the weather
at sea.

"Face up to the way things are,"
she says in a no-nonsense but
accented English.
"When Papa lost everything
in 1625—the brewery, most of our money—
there was no way he could afford a dowry
for me, not with eight other children too.

Cheaper by far to send me
to de Grebber's workshop
to train as a painter
I was in seventh heaven
I can tell you.

Another three months
and I would have been
married off to a banker

twice my age with cross
eyes and no chin.

Not a good fate for a
portrait painter.
As it turned out
I was fully qualified
in the Haarlem Guild
at the age of twenty four.
You see—
bankruptcy saved me.

Forget about what isn't
there anymore.
Take your good right
hand and write."

EAMON'S DRAGONS

Lately I have been looking
at the dragon collection.
There is the placid puppet
dragon. Green body
red eyes, tail, almost
fluffy. Mouth scarlet
which opens two
finger lengths.
Toothless. I move the jaws,
a mouth swallows
a world.
I handle the wooden
dragon delicately.
Its light bones
a precise sculpture.
I could count them
but certainty would
spoil it.
Its tail traces
its past.
There is the paper dragon.
Vivid blues, reds, yellows.
Fully made, it could
span the room.
Finally, the kite
dragon. Its light
plastic lifts
its many greens
to sky.
But there hasn't been
wind for weeks.
It lies in stillness
in a drawer
waiting.

MISSING

Some days I think
I've been here too long
like a tangle of shorthand
no one has the skill to unlock.

Stopping in the middle
of the room I glance at
the mirrored cupboard—
a series of me
in an instant Picasso—
Woman Fragmented.

Now timelessness frays my days,
weeks, months.
Even if solitude heightens pain,
I seek it more and more.
Yet, I do not want to settle
for resignation.
The small details of each day
are what sees me through.

On days I'm not myself
I ventriloquise.
Strange, how few notice
the difference.

I bring slow deliberation
to movement and words.

Run rehearsals in my head
before such outings.
Am alert to all
possible ambushes.

Each sound, an echo
from before—
before, before, before,
before I had to think

of cells seriously—

at four in the morning,
that wakeful hour
when others sleep
but alertness claims me.

Then sleep journeys
me through days, weeks, months.

How odd that it's already
another spring or summer.

I'm not ready yet
for picnic tables
or mid-summer frolics.

I pull closer
to the mirrored cupboard.
In one slight movement I am
one eyed, one breasted, one armed.

Pulling back, I've
two heads, four hands.
I twirl a dance
and become a troupe,
all widemouthed smiles.

Who knows what's missing now?
Just me.

THE HAMMOCK

All summer long
it hung
the hammock
between the poplar
and the cherry.
A wet summer
for the most part.
Between showers
my son dived
onto it
shrieking his claim.
From my cabin,
I heard the creak
creak of his
swaying.
It alarmed the spaces
between the words
my pen awaited.
Other times, I had to resist
its slow rhythm as my hand
raced thoughts
across the page.
There were maybe
a dozen nights
where we sat
around the garden
table with charcoaled
chicken or fish
intent on eating
outside just
because the rain
had stopped.
My cabin light
threw shadows
on its fretwork
as it barely swayed
nobody

pushing it.
Now, that it's
November
and the cherry
and the poplar
leaves lie rotted
in mounds
beneath
its windy
belly
I climb
onto it,
body
muffled
in cap
scarf
gloves
and swing,
the lone
conductor
of the stars.

MUTE

If I were mute
I would not have
to answer that banal
but deadly question—
"How are you?"

If I were mute
I could nod or shake
my head, smile,
frown, be done in seconds
and continue to daydream.

DAUGHTERHOOD

Daughterhood:
it lasts all your life,
even when they're gone--
then especially.

CONFINED

Dada,
confined to bed
a leg opened from
hip to heel
and stitched again.
Your foot a balloon
of pus that must
be cleared three
times a day.
The leg is caged.
I peer in at it
checking that you
keep the toes moving.

You no longer
read a newspaper.
I read you
the Catechism
(your choice)
and feed you
tit-bits of family
gossip in between
the small mouthfuls
of pulped pear.
Your ulcered mouth
is raw-red.
Your teeth in a glass.

You miss the man
who shared your
room till noon
though you did
not know him
four days ago.
You, who have
been ready for
death for years
watch the blossom
sway on the laburnum

from your hospital
window and sing
in an almost whisper,
"Oh Mary, we crown you
with blossoms today,
queen of the angels
queen of the May."

BLINDS

Your ancient memories are immediate,
raw as this summer wind which keeps
the vertical hospital blinds in constant
movement in your room.

Your dreams of the past are real.
Surfacing again and again after
each injection. You hold family
ghosts close in a soft chorus
of remembrance I'm too young to share.

Nevertheless, you name and re-name
them like a travelling song where one
verse is enough to keep on the move.
Your face is yellow-white, stretched over bone,
your frail skull thrown into prominence
in a face without teeth.

I remember my mother move
from stove to table where you
sat drinking tea, your copper
face under a straw hat as you
read summer obituaries
from the paper with cheerful resignation.

SLOWER

Slower, thinner
each time I come there's
less of you.
But even that's not
true all of the time.
Your last heart attack
should have taken you
but you gave it the two fingers
not even remembering it.
Four days later
your face had new flesh.
You were looking forward
to summer.
You moved your toes
like a serious
athlete, counting
the repetitions,
a gold star patient,
a credit to matron.

WHITE SCARS

Still a long way
from white scars,
we both watch your
stitches, brown
and jagged as
they mark you
like drunken
railway tracks.
I am tempted
to align them
as if that's possible.
My hand held mid
-air, hesitant, aware
of not quite appropriate
curiosity.
Instead, I describe
the weather on
the east coast
I've left.

SILENT HANDS

Dada, eighty-five this year.
Not a bad year.
Not like last
when you terrified yourself
and all around you
as your heart gave way.
Then you were solicitous of nurses
craven to doctors
wanting to be home
as soon as they had saved you
in case they changed their minds.

For years, you who had said,
"God rest him, he's in heaven,"
after you had sung full-
throated at other people's
funerals, didn't mention
God at all.

You said nothing
as machines
pinged out your progress,
each of your silent hands
held by a daughter.

THE PIANO

Rogers and Son, London
made the piano a long
time ago.

It had already stood
in the garage for seven
years.

As if waiting
in Biblical time,
and it came to pass

when we took turf
from the garage
or reached a shelf

for a tin of paint
or piece of string
it reminded us

of the tunes
that Dada played.
"I'll Take You Home Again, Kathleen,"

"Abide With Me,"
"Adeste Fidelis"
"The Old Bog Road."

Sometimes I went
back into the house
with my turf basket still

empty to play his tunes,
to replay memory
on the second piano

in the living room.
better tuned
and free from dust.

Still, the piano I hear
is Dada's piano
in the garage.

A day came
when it had to leave.
It was clear he no longer

needed it as he was
seven and a half years
dead.

A painful code
of dismemberment
could be heard

from every room
in the house. At last
Dada's piano was

no longer in the garage
but bedded down
in the skip for the night.

It was not allowed
rest for long.
Two travellers came

into the yard
and said,"There's
a fine piece of stuff

in that. Sure we knew
your father well.
He wouldn't begrudge us."

RUNAWAY GIRL

1

I did not catch a chameleon.
The elders did.
They beat the dried skin
mixed it with the secret potion.
They made of our faces
a green mask.

Beauty, they called it
but I was watchful.
When we moved through the forest
or swam in the wide rivers,
our heads held above water
eyes turned to sky
I knew we were not blue of the river
or green of tree branches.
I felt only my neck twisted.

My cousin spoke in my ear,
"Stop your ugly words.
You insult the chameleon.
Your neck is gold-stretched
to beauty. Seven rings,
swim, smile."

And what could I do?
The red flood had broken through.
The time had come, the time had come.
The elders knew all ceremonies.

To be picked first.
First bride from the river
bank. To be pulled from water
by him whose lips curl
darkly in kohl.
Also, his eyes, the whites
of teeth, white pillars
to be prized.

My head fell to water.
The chameleon fled
washed by water spirits.
I could not now be chosen.
I doubted.
My head drooped.
That is all.

When the wise one
shaved my head
and buried the troubled hairs
under the eucalyptus,
when my ancestors' bones beat shame
at the night feast,
when my father's eyes measured
my skeleton and my mother's back
spoke silence...
I knew their tent was full
without me.

The night came.
I followed the river.
I would not look back.

In the morning forest
drenched in light,
leaves dancing for the monkeys,
I ate nuts, whistled
like a boy-son.

2.
I did not know the pearl
was poisoned, like a blaze
of black at the centre of the poppy.

The pearl
all mine, they said
if I would drink.

They beat drums.
My father's eyes housed mine
but my mother's fell to the bowl.

I would not drink.
Their drums beat
on me until my eyes met night.

At the edge of the forest
leaves dancing to monkeys
I woke, my body blue
with pain.

A girl sang like a boy-son.

3.
The red flow comes
again and again.
I watch it.
Its richness is all mine.
 No man will stop it now.

My steps have left him
behind.
His silver flow
covers another. It is the way.

The bone-drums
will beat their joining. Her neck
so tall
it will reach
the sky.

His silver flow
will drown her
in boy-children.
As the sun rises
and sets
her womb

will count
its swellings

4.
The birds are silent.
The hairs of the sacred one
no longer come in visions.
His changing shapes
are withheld from me.

Not to see him
in naked trees
or sky angered
to thunder,
that is my punishment.
Yet, in his absence,
I wear red feathers.

I have become alert
to crocodile and scorpion.
My steps are mine alone.

I wear golden rings
in my ears.
On days when there is
nothing to eat
I feed on colours to come.
I sit to flames
of my own making.

5.
Who are the partners of speech?
Not the elders.
Not my brothers.
Sometimes, after darkness
when the trees whistle
a silence only I can hear,

I listen to my sisters' voices,
but they are faint.

Lower than a whisper.
I listen hard
but I cannot hear.
The trees silence them.

I am stern with my steps,
not to walk backwards
once more into wind
which blows only darkness.
When I lay in the lotus
my lover's silver
flooding me,
I could not see the whites
of his teeth, the fire of his eyes.
I saw only the elders
with their collars of skulls,
watching me, watching us.

He whispered tales
of the lion and serpent
but I told him
I would no longer eat
fire for ancestors.

We offered food to the sacred
bones heaped to sky-mountain.
They did not answer.

6
The leaves have left
the trees.
Heaven is naked
and the monkeys have fled.
The air curves in coldness.

I shiver and long for my parents' tent.
My feet know they cannot follow that wish.
There was a time when daylight was endless.

Winter gods are savage.
Each day I dig a water hole.
Sometimes, there is no water.
Then I drink my tears.
For some time I hunched in a cave
but the bears returned.

Breathless in the undergrowth
I wanted to lean on my parents'
totem pole, to lie against the carved
figures of my ancestors.

To dip my fingers in my mother's
pot and fill my father's pipe.
On those days, I heard nothing
but my sobs.

My body twisted with them
until they became drumbeats
of pain. I listened,
then I stopped.
What are these sobs?
Drumbeats in my body and my head?

The naked forest listened
to my questions.
It did not answer
but I waited.

When night closed on
 my questions, my heart opened.
It said, "Your sobs are not drumbeats.
They are the
liquid perfume of your pain."

7.
I walk straight,
tall as trees.
Flights of birds
kick my heels to sun, sky.

A strange newness is mine.
The sky curves to my eye.
My pains are open.

My shadow life
has ended.
To be free from drum-beats,
that is my relief.

I am sister to monkeys
and friend of birds.
Our songs are one.

COBWEBS

All day I've been fishing for cobwebs
in this, my mother's house, street-bound
from the front and from the back cliff-edged
over river and racecourse.

Alive, the Hausfrau in her never let spiders
rest in a corner. Since she went, they take
advantage of my idleness: the occasional visitor,
who still comes home to mother; she's not here,
though her house takes care of me.

I make lists now, as she did when my life was too impatient
for all but endless forward motion:
paint the peeling window, clear the gutter
sweep up mulched leaves in wet Autumn.
Reflection then meant only my blurred image in a mirror.

Here I can sit for hours and listen to wind strip the trees
or pigeons splat the window glass.
All action or inertia: the twin poles of my being
at "Island View".

The family tale needs more than
a single voice to search its secrets.
What grounds me here to place and person:
that hunt for memory and memory withheld.

HER HANDS

My mother had clever hands
making patchwork quilts, children's clothes,
bread, scones, cakes.

My first memory is of those hands
lifting me to sky, never to feel as exhilarated
or safe again.

Those hands,
the cathedral of my childhood.

In my teens I scoffed at her housewifery.
Her favourite word was wife.

Her hands, the practical
romance of the marriage.

My father's hands in clouds
only she could see.

MY HANDS

I made my hands awkward.
I forbade them the domestic
language of stove and sewing.

I observed my mother's
excellence at both
and forced my fingers

to stutter when I held
a bowl or glass.
Surrounded by fragments

I was pushed aside
and sent to put order
on the linen cupboard.

I enjoyed putting new
labels on shelves
twice a year.

       2.

Amo   Amamus
Amas   Amatis
Amat   Amant
And I did,
my Latin Primer
proudly held
in my twelve year old hands.

I rattled it off for my grandmother
after my first day in the big school.
"You've a great way with words," she said
and put extra honey on my scone.

"Her mouth is fast but her hands are slow,"
my mother said through a mouthful of pins.
Her legs danced on the treadle of the Singer
sewing machine. Her hands guided a hem.

INTERVAL ACT

My mother made
my tartan skirt.
Pleated, the two halters
crossed my back.
The white blouse
stiffly starched.
A ribbon spanned my head.

Heavy dancing shoes
hornpiped my delight,
their shiny buckles
flinging silver dreams
across the stage.
We were the interval act.

Daly's Dancing School
at the City Theatre.
Front page news
on the local paper.

Now this yellowed photo
lies in my mother's box.
My smile is wide
but my eyes closed
on the flash.

Only I can see
the silver buckles now.
The picture ends at the knees.

LENT

Lent came.
My father weighed eggs.
My hunger grew.

A street dog opened
my freckled face.
I fasted,
stood guard over words
not letting them onto paper.

Simeon on a high stone,
I read dictionaries
in my favourite tree.

HOME ECONOMICS

"Give up Home Economics!
Is that wise?" Dada asks,
"Sister Pascal says it
would be utter foolishness
and I'm inclined to agree."

He bites into Mama's
fresh scones.
It's early Saturday
morning.
She baked them
still in her nurse's uniform
when she came in after night duty.

COOKBOOKS
AND SOAP

When my mother died
there was enough soap
to last the household
for years
amongst other things:
yachting varnish
to protect the windows
--for three years
red sealant for the outhouses
--six years.
Assorted jams
--two years.
A box of locks, forever
if you were careful
and didn't lose the keys.
Two shelves of cookbooks
and notebooks.
I boxed those
immediately.
Others had borrowed them.
She had used them rarely.
Marguerite Patten had taught
her how to make do with
whatever ingredients were
to hand, as a youthful
nurse in the London Blitz.
She could never throw
away string or paper bags
though her house was always
too tidy for my taste.
My favourite photo shows her
propped lengthwise on a couch
supported by a cushion.

At rest at last,
you might think.
But no, when I
scrutinize the picture
I see her hands
are busy
embroidering a cover.

MAMA AT REST

I have been searching
for photos of my mother
at her ease.

So many boxes
of family snaps
from which she's
absent.

Busy at the edges
of things though
she provided the largesse
on show—
A table filled
with the debris
of a good dinner,
the treat of the
as yet uncut
birthday cake
alight
in festive sweetness.

This very summer
she is fifteen years dead.
Only yesterday
I spent the afternoon
cutting the grass
on her grave.
"Keeping it in order,"
she would have said.

EYRIE

When we moved
to our high eyrie
overlooking the city
belled by cathedrals
we danced
on blonde floorboards
marvelled
at windows
best left undressed,
air, light,
light, air --
lightheaded
even in sleep
we danced
in our blonde bed.

Now we are the roof
of our building,
not quite eyeball to eyeball
with the weathervane
on Christchurch Cathedral.
Waking at dawn
to re-discover
our newfound land,
alert to the silence
of the bells,
we looked towards
the parapeted bridge
to mark
the progress
of a lone
reveller.